ROXIE MUNRO

WILD WEST TRAIL RIDE MAZE

b
BRIGHT SKY PRESS
ALBANY, TEXAS

Trail Ride Rules

JOIN COWBOYS ON A TRAIL RIDE!

FIND YOUR WAY

From Crooked River Ranch headquarters to the cattle pens out on the range, and the cowboy's camp, and then wind your way back home to the ranch again, on a different path.

PLAY THE ABC GAME

There's a hidden letter shape on each page, starting with A on the first page and ending with Z on the last. Find something on each page that begins with that letter (on the first page, something that starts with "A," on the second page "B," and so on).

IN EACH MAZE

Find eight cowboys on the path out to the pens, and find them coming back home again on the return path to the ranch.

How many times on the trip do the cowboys ford a river?

Check out the "Remuda" — spare horses brought along for the cowboys.

Where's the chuckwagon on the way out, and where is it on the way back?

To help the Crooked River cowboys keep track of the herd, count the cattle along the way.

Find Charlie the cook.

Look for "Cloud," the white horse.

Look out for the wily coyote — he's in each maze.

HAVE FUN!

Answers begin on page 30.

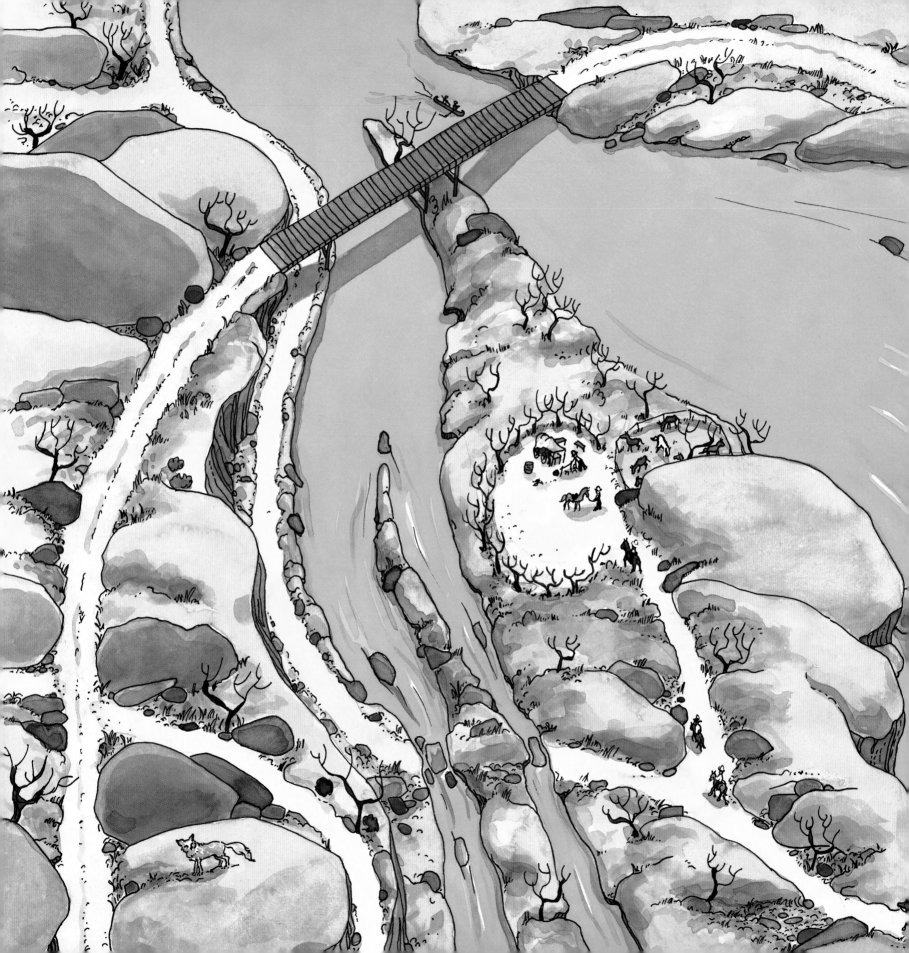

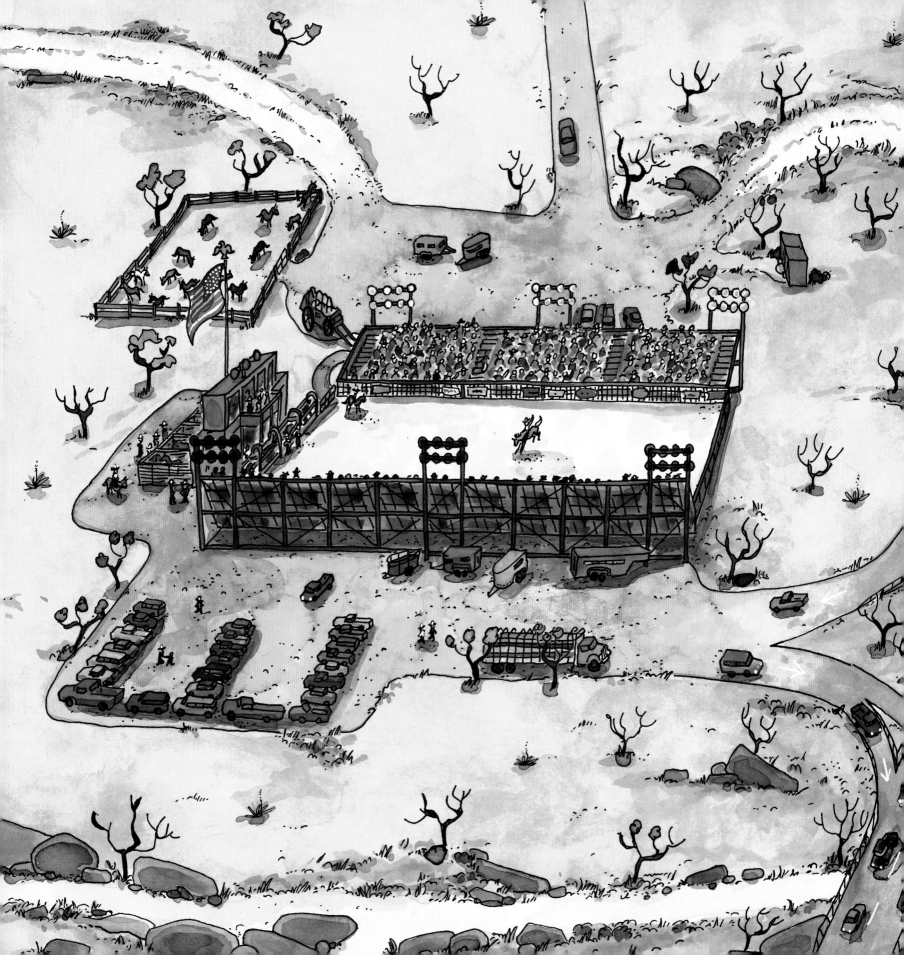

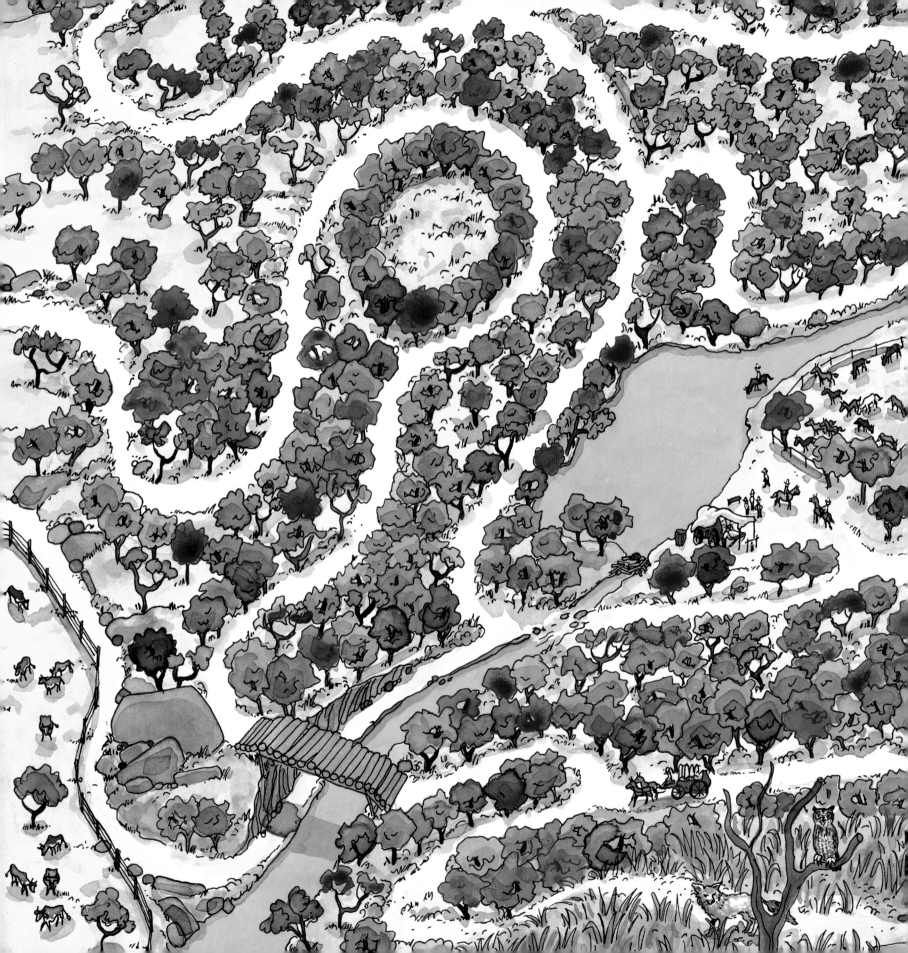

ANSWER KEY

Headquarters

A for Armadillo
B for Buffalo
River Fords: 1
Cattle: 0

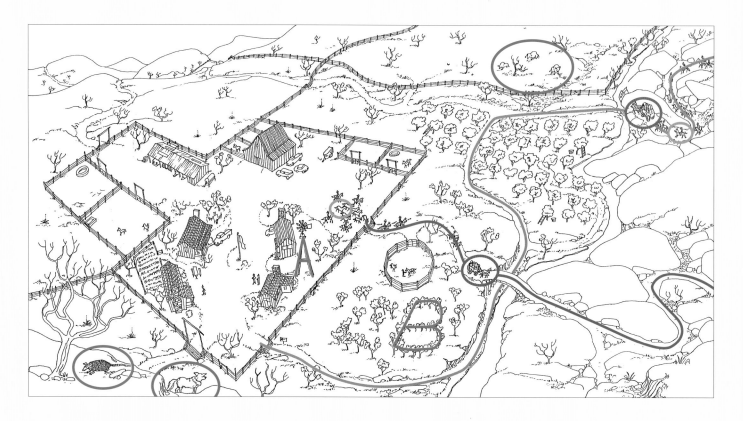

River

C for Canoe
D for Deer
River Fords: 2
Cattle: 0

Rodeo

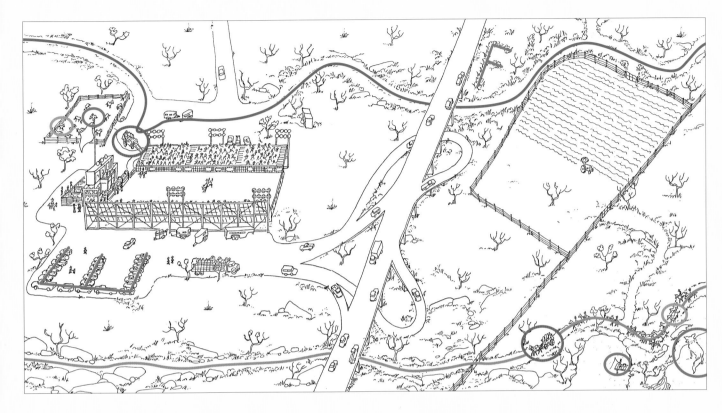

E for Eagle
F for Fisherman
River Fords: 0
Cattle: 0

Old West Town

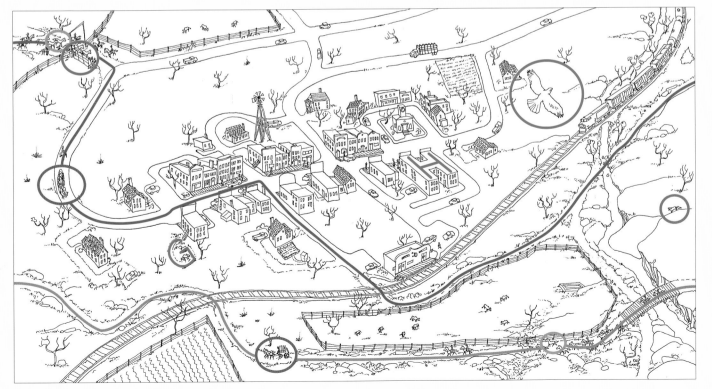

G for Gate
H for Hawk
River Fords: 1
Cattle: 11

ANSWER KEY

Mountains

I for Island
J for Jackrabbit
River Fords: 3
Cattle: 0

Canyons

K for Kayak
L for Ladder
River Fords: 0
Cattle: 7

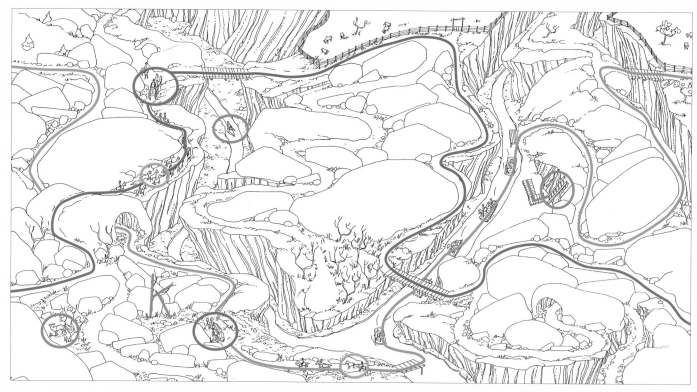

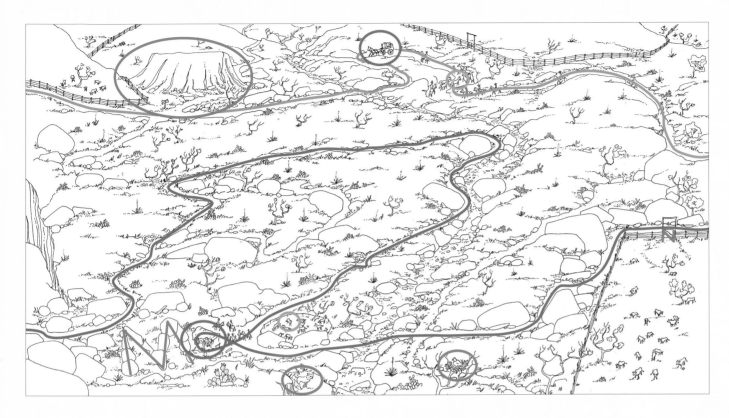

Prairie

M for Mesa
N for Nest
River Fords: 0
Cattle: 25

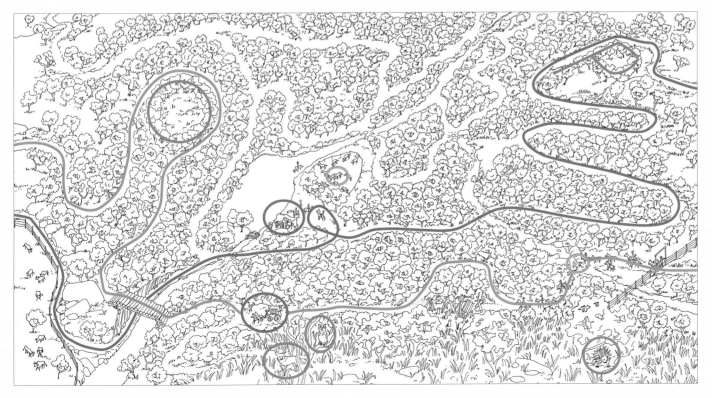

Forest

O for Owl
P for Porcupine
River Fords: 3
Cattle: 9

ANSWER KEY

Grasslands

Q for Quail
R for Rattlesnake
River Fords: 2
Cattle: 13

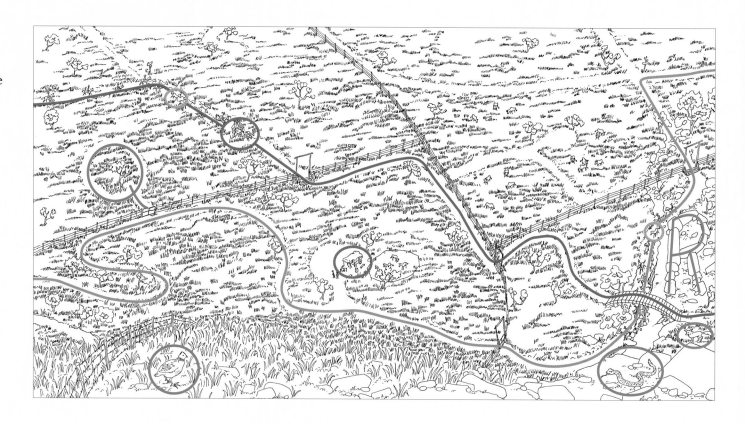

Pond

S for Sheep
T for Turkey
River Fords: 2
Cattle: 12

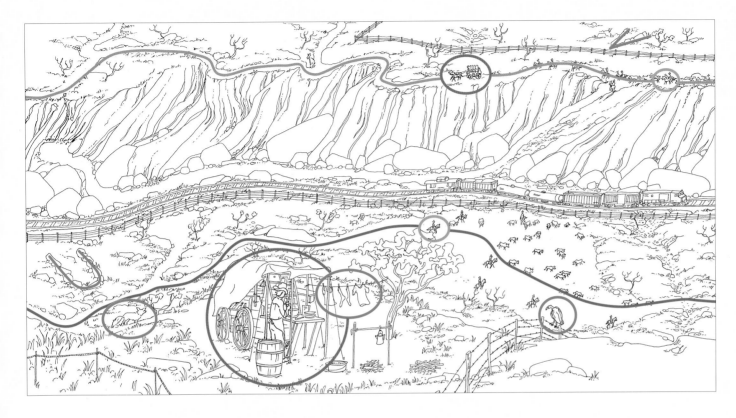

Roundup

U for Underwear
V for Vulture
River Fords: 0
Cattle: 30

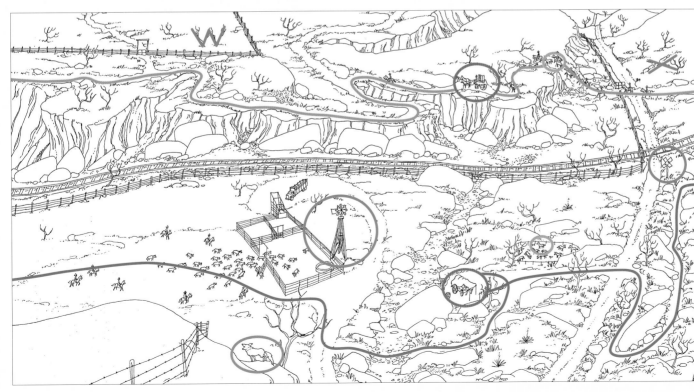

Pens

W for Windmill
X for Railroad
     Crossing
River Fords: 0
Cattle: 34

ANSWER KEY

Camp

Y for Yoke
Z for Zigzag
River Fords: 4
Cattle: 22

Answer Color Guide

— Way Out
— Way Back
— Coyote
— Cloud
— Charlie the Cook
& Chuckwagon
— Hidden Letters
& Hidden Item

To my nephew, Aaron Munro Wood.

b BRIGHT SKY PRESS
Albany, Texas

Copyright © 2005 by Roxie Munro

10   9 8 7 6 5 4 3 2 1

Library of Congress Cataloging-in-Publication Data

Munro, Roxie.
The Wild West trail ride maze / by Roxie Munro.
p. cm.
ISBN 1-931721-67-X (alk. paper)
1. Maze puzzles—Juvenile literature.   2. West (U.S.)—Juvenile literature.
3. Cowboys—West (U.S.)—Juvenile literature. I. Title.

GV1507.M3 M88 2006
793.73'8—dc22

2005045687

Book and jacket design by Julie Savasky

Printed in China